Dear Parents and Educators,

Welcome to Penguin Young Readers! As parents and educators, you know that each child develops at his or her own pace—in terms of speech, critical thinking, and, of course, reading. Penguin Young Readers recognizes this fact. As a result, each Penguin Young Readers book is assigned a traditional easy-to-read level (1–4) as well as a Guided Reading Level (A–P). Both of these systems will help you choose the right book for your child. Please refer to the back of each book for specific leveling information. Penguin Young Readers features esteemed authors and illustrators, stories about favorite characters, fascinating nonfiction, and more!

Thomas Edison and His Bright Idea

LEVEL **3**

GUIDED
READING
LEVEL **K**

This book is perfect for a **Transitional Reader** who:
- can read multisyllable and compound words;
- can read words with prefixes and suffixes;
- is able to identify story elements (beginning, middle, end, plot, setting, characters, problem, solution); and
- can understand different points of view.

Here are some **activities** you can do during and after reading this book:
- Creative Writing: Pretend you are an inventor. Write a journal entry about your ideas for inventions. What will they do? What problems will they solve?
- -ed Endings: List all the words in the story that have an -ed ending. On a separate piece of paper, write the root word next to the word with the -ed ending. The chart below will get you started:

word with an -ed ending	root word
asked	ask
peeked	peek
piled	pile

Remember, sharing the love of reading with a child is the best gift you can give!

—Bonnie Bader, EdM
  Penguin Young Readers program

*Penguin Young Readers are leveled by independent reviewers applying the standards developed by Irene Fountas and Gay Su Pinnell in *Matching Books to Readers: Using Leveled Books in Guided Reading*, Heinemann, 1999.

To Aodhan and Aneka,
for their bright curiosity and wonder—PBD

PENGUIN YOUNG READERS
An Imprint of Penguin Random House LLC

Text copyright © 2016 by Patricia Brennan. Illustrations copyright © 2016 by Jez Tuya. All rights reserved.
Published by Penguin Young Readers, an imprint of Penguin Random House LLC, 345 Hudson Street,
New York, New York 10014. Manufactured in China.

Library of Congress Cataloging-in-Publication Data is available.

ISBN 978-0-448-48830-1 (pbk)   10 9 8 7 6 5 4 3 2
ISBN 978-0-448-48831-8 (hc)   10 9 8 7 6 5 4 3 2 1

Thomas Edison
and His Bright Idea

by Patricia Brennan Demuth
illustrated by Jez Tuya

Penguin Young Readers
An Imprint of Penguin Random House

Who was Thomas Edison?

He was an inventor.

An inventor thinks up new ideas.

Thomas had a very *bright* idea.

His idea lit up the world!

Thomas Alva Edison was born in 1847.

Little Tom always asked questions.

How does this work?

What's inside here?

One day, Tom saw falling grain.

Where did it go?

Tom went up the bin ladder.

He peeked over the side—

and fell in!

Grain piled over Tom!

He was pulled out

just in time.

Tom began school in a
one-room schoolhouse.
The teacher said
Tom wasn't too bright.
His questions were silly.

Mrs. Edison got mad.

She knew her boy was smart.

After that, she taught Tom at home.

Tom soon learned to read.
Books gave him answers
to all his questions.
So Tom read one book
after another.
"I didn't read a few books,"
he said later.
"I read the library!"

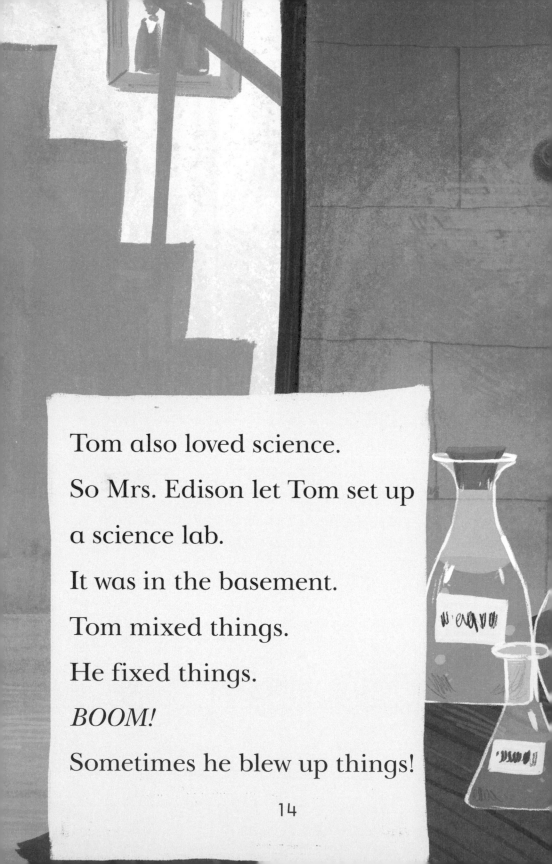

Tom also loved science.

So Mrs. Edison let Tom set up

a science lab.

It was in the basement.

Tom mixed things.

He fixed things.

BOOM!

Sometimes he blew up things!

Tom's family did not have
much money.
So young Tom got a job on a train.
He was just 12.

But Tom wanted to keep learning.

His boss let him use

one of the train cars.

Tom set up a lab inside!

Tom grew up and got other jobs.

One day at work,

a machine stopped running.

No one could fix it.

Then Tom walked by.

He could take things apart.

And he could put them

back together.

Soon Tom fixed the old machine.

Then he invented a new one!

It worked great!

Tom sold it for a lot of money.

What did Tom do with his money?

He set up a big science lab.

And he hired lots of workers.

Edison was now a full-time inventor.

He could dream up new things
all day long.

Tom was very, very busy.
Before long, he needed
a bigger place.
So he moved to
Menlo Park, New Jersey.
He built a brand-new lab.

Tom drew his ideas on paper.

His helpers looked at the drawings.

Then they set to work with tools.
Soon Tom's ideas turned into
useful new things!

Back then, people had to copy pages by hand.

So Tom invented a copy machine.

The telephone was new at that time.

It was hard to hear callers

on the other end.

So Tom invented something

to make sounds louder.

Next, Tom tried to catch sound.

He made a special roller

covered with tinfoil.

Tom turned the roller with a crank.

"Mary had a little lamb," he said.

A needle made marks on the tinfoil.

Tom turned the crank again.

The roller talked back!

"Mary had a little lamb," it said.

Tom had recorded sound!

The new invention was called a
phonograph (say FONE-a-graff).
It made Tom very famous.

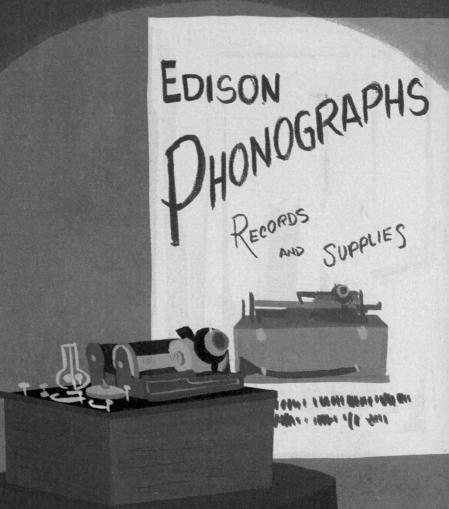

His inventions seemed like magic.
People called Tom a wizard—
"the Wizard of Menlo Park."

Tom often worked day and night.

Midnight came.

But Tom didn't go to bed.

He was too happy working.

During the day,

he took naps on a bench.

One day, Tom set a new goal:

to make an electric light.

The light had to turn off and on.

Back then, people used fire for light.

They lit lamps inside.

And they lit lamps outside.

Other inventors had tried to make electric lights.
But they all failed.

Some lights were way too bright.

Others weren't bright enough.

Some lights went out right away.

Tom set to work on his new idea.

He used a battery for power.

He used a glass globe for a bulb.

But what should he put inside

the glass?

That was the hard part.

What would get hot enough to glow

without burning up?

He put fishing line inside the bulb.

Then he hooked it to power.

A light glowed inside.

But it soon went out.

Tom tried putting other things
inside the bulb.
Then one day, Tom used
sewing thread coated with soot.
This time the light glowed for
one hour . . . two hours . . .
three hours!
The light glowed on and on.
Tom had done it!
He had invented
an electric lightbulb—
one that really worked!

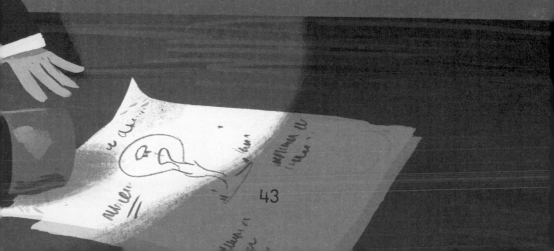

On New Year's Eve 1879,
Tom showed off his new light.
Thousands of people took the train
to Menlo Park.

The night was dark.

Then Tom pulled a switch.

Lights came on everywhere!

It was amazing!

Today, Tom's bright lights are everywhere!
Tom lit up our world.

Tom invented more than
1,000 new things.
But the electric lightbulb was
his best invention of all.
Next time you flip on a light,
thank Thomas Edison!